THE DAILY LIFE OF COLONISTS DURING THE REVOLUTIONARY WAR

History Stories for Children | Children's History Books

Speedy Publishing LLC

40 E. Main St. #1156

Newark, DE 19711

www.speedypublishing.com

Copyright 2017

All Rights reserved. No part of this book may be reproduced or used in any way or form or by any means whether electronic or mechanical, this means that you cannot record or photocopy any material ideas or tips that are provided in this book

In this book, we're going to talk about the daily life of colonists during the American Revolutionary War. So, let's get right to it!

BATTLE OF LONG ISLAND

At the beginning of the war, there were about 2.5 million people living in the 13 colonies. About one-fourth of the citizens lived in Virginia, which was the first colony that had been established. Approximately one fifth of the entire population was made up of African-American slaves.

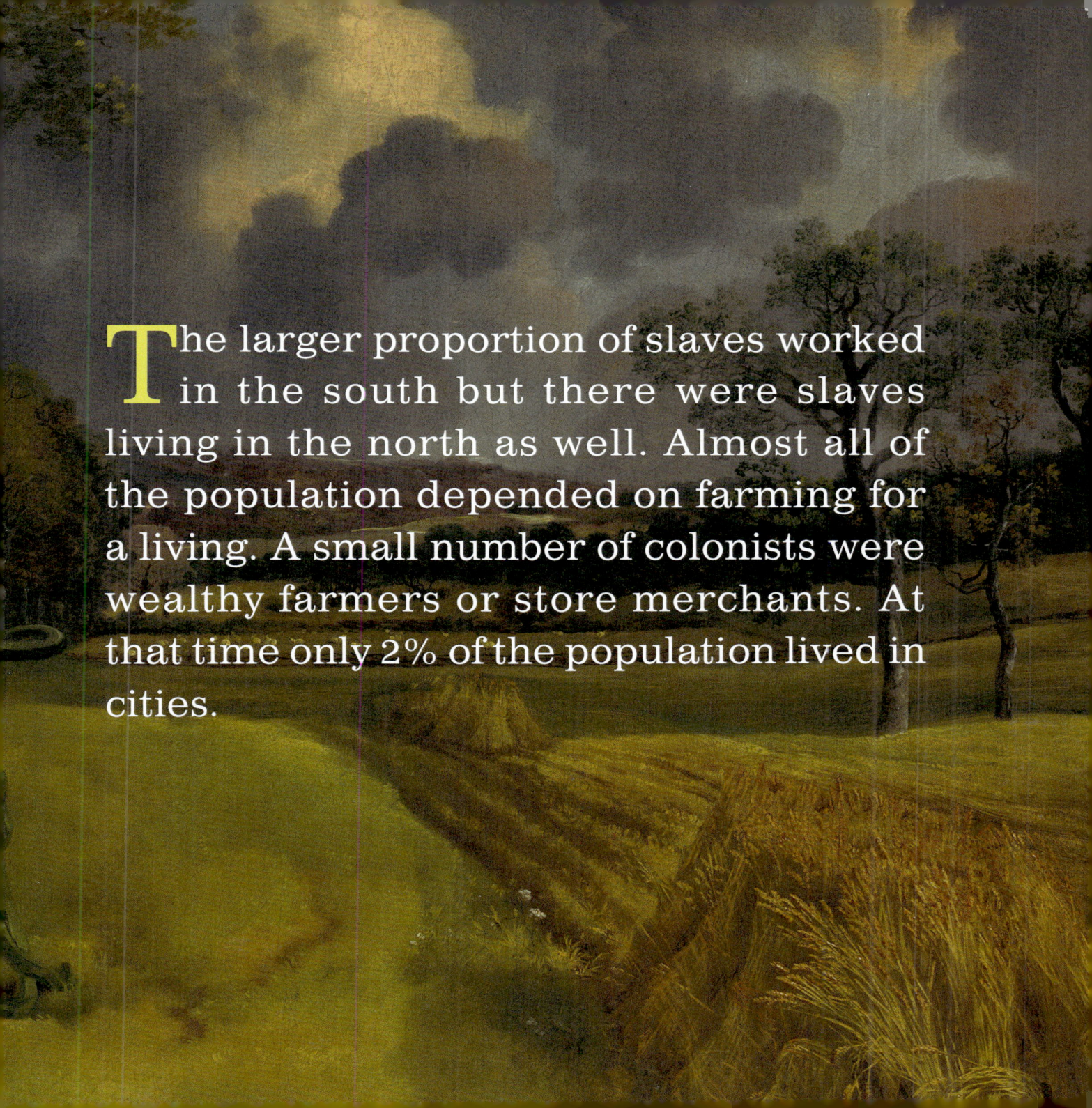

The larger proportion of slaves worked in the south but there were slaves living in the north as well. Almost all of the population depended on farming for a living. A small number of colonists were wealthy farmers or store merchants. At that time only 2% of the population lived in cities.

Those farmers who remained on their farms and didn't fight in the war, were mainly concerned with getting enough food

to feed their families and fighting off any marauders who invaded their lands.

A RESIDENCE AT THE RED RIVER COLONY

IN WHAT KINDS OF HOMES DID THE FREE COLONISTS LIVE?

Just like today, the kinds of homes that people lived in reflected their wealth. Most families were poor or middle class. Wealthy families were rare.

A typical family would have been a family of four or six with a mother, father, and children. Sometimes older relatives may have lived with them too. They often lived in a one- or two-room house that was about the same size as today's garages, about 16 feet by 20 feet.

HOLT HOUSEN BUILT BEFORE 1800

The houses were frequently constructed from wood. There was usually a fireplace with a chimney for burning wood to keep warm. Some homes had floors made of wood, but others just had dirt floors. The kitchen was sometimes built separately from the rest of the house to prevent fires. If the farmer had slaves working for him, they lived in nearby outbuildings or shacks.

The homes didn't have plumbing or electricity like today's homes and had to use candles and the fireplace for light. Those who were wealthy lived in two-story houses that sometimes had four downstairs rooms as well as two rooms upstairs. The very wealthy lived in mansions.

18TH CENTURY HOUSE

A GIRL HOLDING HER HORNBOOK.

HOW DID KIDS LEARN?

The mothers in colonial homes took care of infants and children. Children between the ages of 6 and 8 were taught their letters and sometimes how to read the Bible. To learn their letters, children carried a hornbook. The hornbook had a page with the alphabet or religious text. This page was covered over with a thin transparent sheet of mica, called horn.

It was attached to a frame with a handle. The hornbook had been around as a teaching tool since 1450 in England. The New England primer was another type of book that was used to help children learn to read. Each letter of the alphabet had a rhyme to make it easier to learn.

    Not all kids attended school. In the northern colonies more attended school than in the south. Many were taught at home. If his parents could read, a young boy was taught how to read, how to write, and how to do basic arithmetic. He was expected to run the farm or conduct business when he got older.

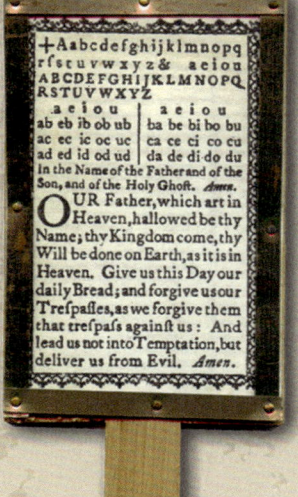
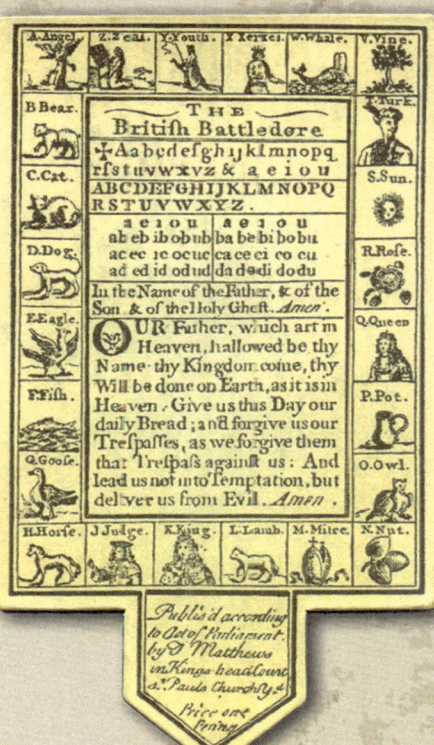

HORNBOOKS

AN 18TH CENTURY GIRL

Young girls sometimes learned to read and write, but they were also taught how to prepare meals and how to sew since they were expected to take care of households and raise children when they got older. Wealthy children may have had a few books in their homes, such as a volume of Aesop's Fables.

WHAT TYPE OF CLOTHING DID THEY WEAR?

A closet filled with clothes only happened in the homes of the wealthy. Most farming families only had two or three changes of clothing for each family member. Bathing was a luxury that only took place a few times a year. The clothes they wore were mostly made at home by the women in the family.

TYPICAL 18TH CENTURY FEMALE CLOTHING

18TH CENTURY CLOTHING

The women wore dresses with long skirts, which they covered with aprons when they were cooking. On their heads they wore mob caps. These were bonnets made of cloth that had pleats and a brim that was ruffed. Young women wore similar clothes.

The men's dress-up clothing consisted of breeches, a type of pants that were tied under the knee. They wore stockings with leather shoes and cotton shirts. On their heads they wore triangular-shaped hats called tricorns.

The boys dressed in the same style as their fathers. While working on the farm, they kept their clothing simple. Wealthy people wore powdered wigs and had their clothes imported from England until the blockage prevented clothing imports.

A MAN'S SET OF VELVET CLOTHES, 1755

KITCHEN LIFE 18TH CENTURY

WHAT DID THEY EAT?

Most families in the colonies ate the vegetables and fruits they grew on their farms. They hunted and fished for meat. Their diet was largely meats and seafood accompanied by vegetables and cooked over a slow fire in stews.

The main meal was usually served in the early afternoon because it took so long to get everything ready.

HOW DID THE AMERICAN REVOLUTION AFFECT THE COLONISTS' LIVES?

Most of the colonists weren't actively fighting in the Revolution, but this doesn't mean it didn't affect their lives. Their lives were already difficult and the fighting around their homes and farms just made their lives harder.

GUNPOWDER AND CANNON SMOKE DURING THE BATTLE OF LONG ISLAND

A VIEW OF A FARM HOUSE

However, they still had to farm their crops and complete their daily tasks in order to survive. During those times it was unusual for children to have much schooling past the third grade. After that, they were expected to participate on the farm and their responsibilities increased if their fathers or older brothers were fighting in the war.

Farms that were in the path of armies, either Patriots or Loyalists, were in harm's way. Despite warnings from the military leaders on both sides, soldiers sometimes plundered their lands and stole food, livestock, and other goods that they needed, leaving the farming families in a desperate situation.

A PEASANT FAMILY IN A FARM HOUSE

PHOTO OF A FAMILY IN 18TH CENTURY

Those families who were on the side of the Patriots were in particular danger, since the British sometimes burned down their homes if they found out. At times, when their men were away, women as well as their children and the elderly living with them had no choice when the British arrived at their farms. Their homes or other meeting places were taken over by British soldiers for living quarters, hospitals, and prisons.

WHAT WERE THE ECONOMIC CONSEQUENCES OF THE REVOLUTION?

As the British started to enter the major cities, such as Boston and New York, City dwellers left for the countryside seeking food and places to work. All the traditional ways to sell were affected.

BOSTON MASSACRE

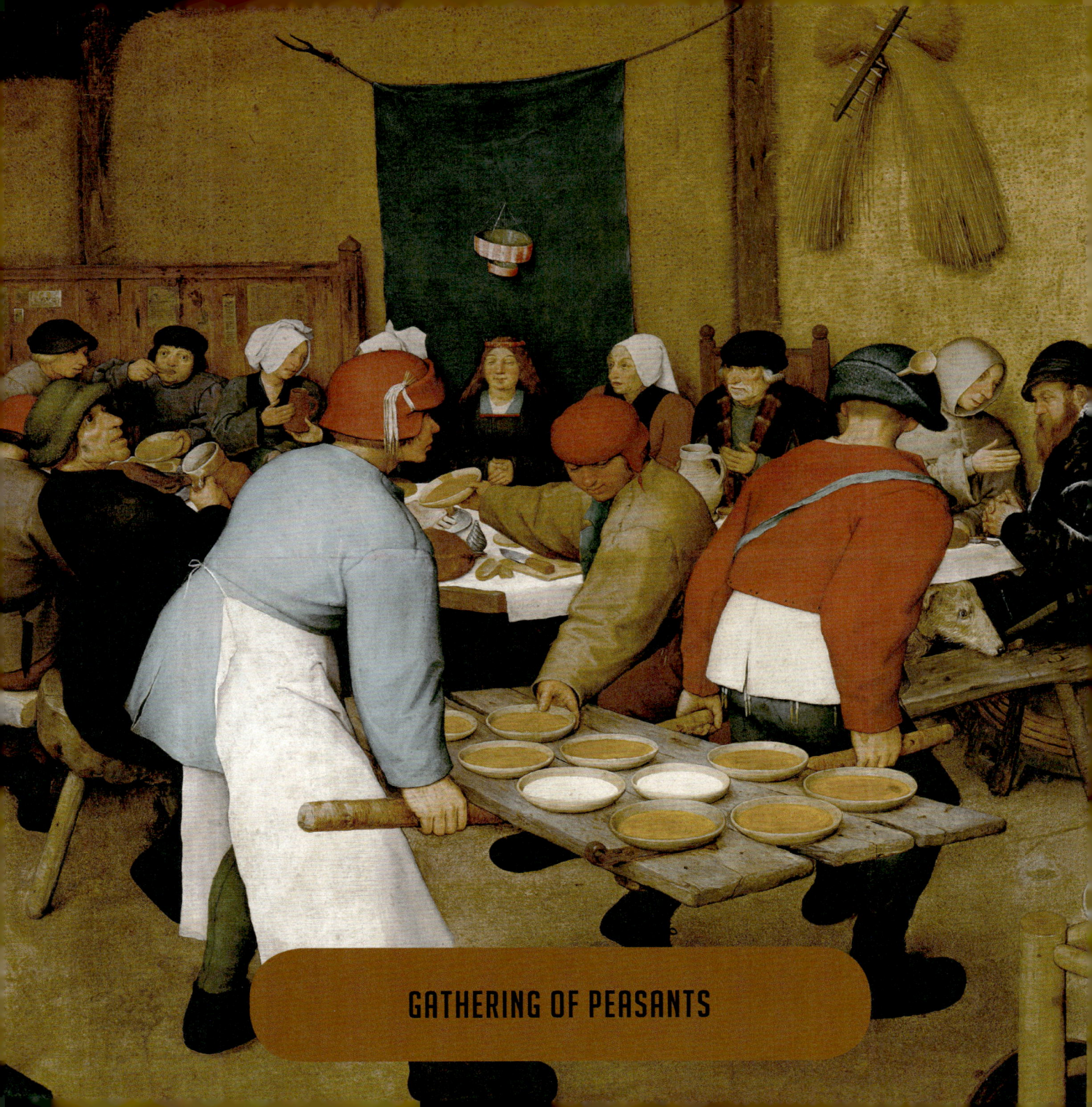

GATHERING OF PEASANTS

Farmers that desperately needed money might be selling their produce to American customers one week and in the next week they might be selling to the British army who had occupied their area.

The blockade of the American coastline by the British had caused massive unemployment. Anyone who had depended on goods coming into the country was out of work from people who were working on the docks to city merchants.

Desperate for food and struggling to survive, many men and women became camp followers and pursued the armies in order to obtain some work and get a hot meal. Of course, even during desperate times there are always some people who try to use circumstances for their own gain.

Scarcity of Food

MILK FARMERS SELLING MILK

Some farmers and store owners who had goods raised their prices because goods were so scarce and the British would pay at the increased prices. These inflationary prices sometimes caused protests and violence from the colonists and Congress had to enact laws to prevent prices from rising too high.

HOW DID THE ROLE OF WOMEN CHANGE DURING THE REVOLUTION?

O The Continental army was largely made up of farmers and merchants who joined in the fight against the British. When these men went off to war, the women stepped up to take their roles.

CONTINENTAL ARMY

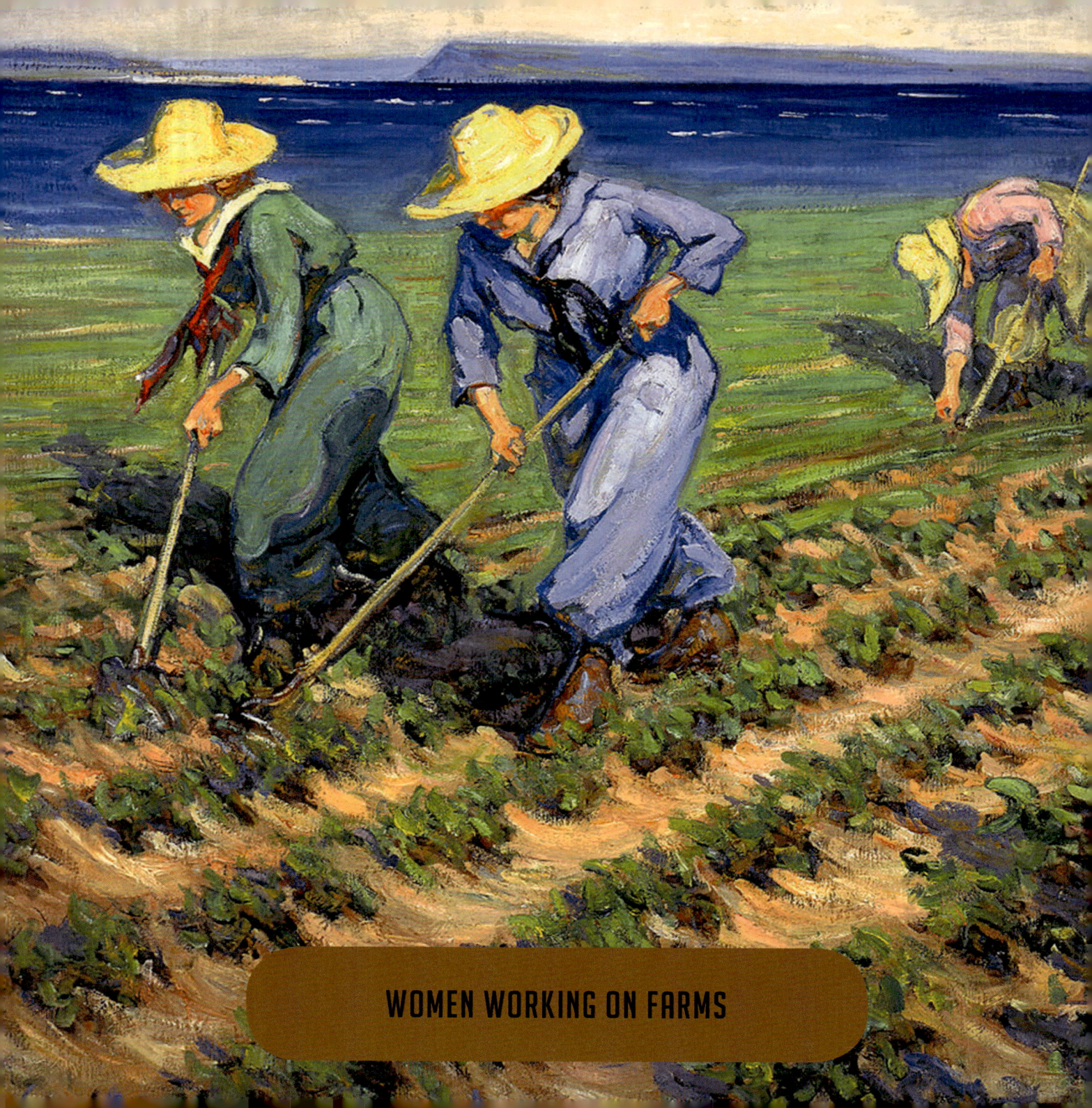

In addition to handling all the household tasks, women were also doing double duty taking care of the men's tasks on farms and businesses. Their children and other relatives helped as well, but it was a very hard life and work took place from sunrise to sunset.

They were also called upon for additional help from neighboring militias. When there was a need for uniforms or food, these women helped the Patriots by sewing homespun clothes and bringing food to them. When British soldiers showed up at their doorsteps, they were often met with a woman holding a gun.

Washington and Lafayette at Valley Forge

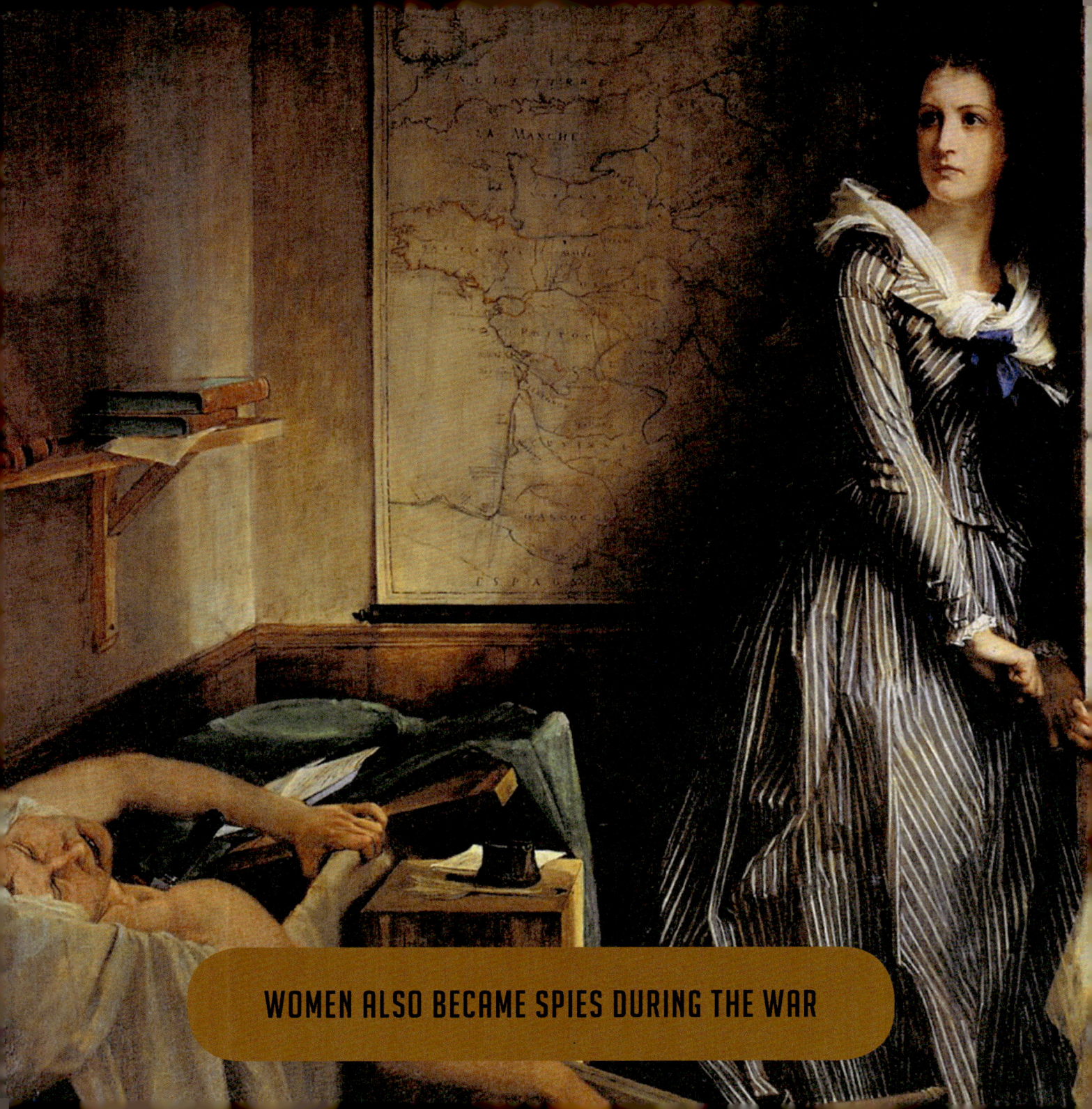

Some women also became spies during the war. Men did not suspect them so they paid attention to what the British were saying and then passed the information on to Washington's army. The men who were lucky enough to survive the war and return to their homes came home to independent women who had frequently saved their farms and businesses from bankruptcy.

DID WOMEN AND CHILDREN SEE THE BATTLES?

The war was fought where the armies met. Often, this was near or on people's farmland. Sometimes farm families would wake up to the sounds of musket shots or cannon firing.

WOMEN NURSING WAR CASUALTIES

WAR DRUMMERS

Boys could enlist as young as 16-years-old. Sometimes boys who were only 7 or 8 years or age joined the army as drummers or as army messenger boys to deliver important messages from place to place.

Awesome! Now you know more about how colonists lived during the Revolutionary War. You can find more History books from Baby Professor by searching the website of your favorite book retailer.

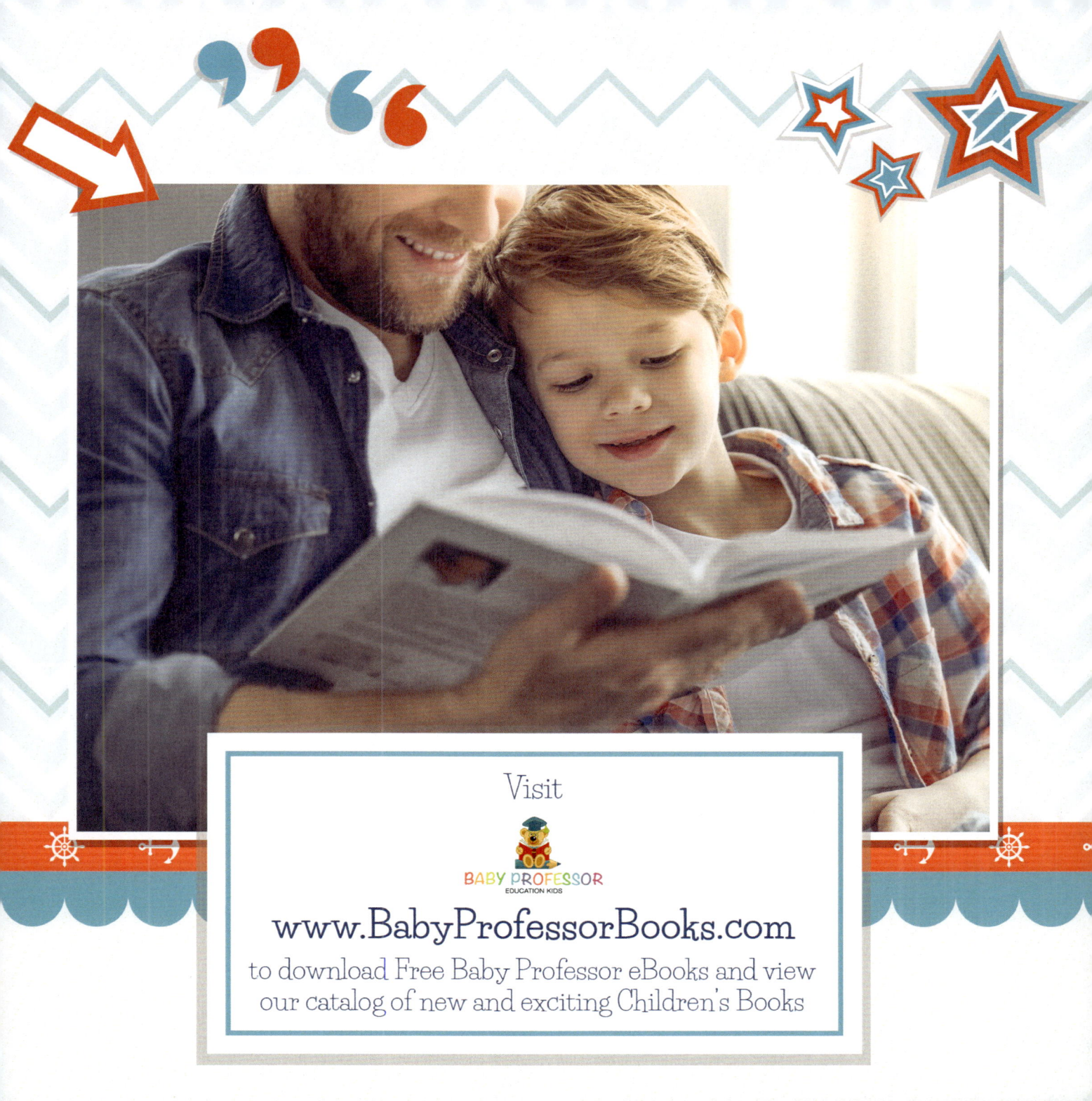

Made in the USA
Middletown, DE
13 September 2017